The Complete

JUNIOR JUDO

The Complete

JUNIOR JUDO

by Mick Leigh, 7th Dan
British Judo Association

Photographs by Paul Keevil, 1st Dan

foulsham
LONDON • NEW YORK • TORONTO • SYDNEY

W. Foulsham & Company Limited
The Publishing House, Bennetts Close,
Cippenham, Slough, Berkshire SL1 4AP

ISBN 0-572-01821-5

First published 1983 as *Junior Judo* 1, 2 and 3

Printed in Great Britain.

Contents

Section One

Section Two

Section Three

Introduction

This book will provide a useful introduction to the many youngsters entering the exciting sport of judo.

Although you can learn a great deal about the sport from this book, you should always study judo under a qualified instructor who will tell you when you are ready to try particular throws and holds, will correct your mistakes, provided detailed individual instruction, and help you if you have problems.

Please remember that because I say something should be done in a certain way, this does not mean it is the only way. Perhaps it may not even be the best way for you. This is one reason why personal instruction in the sport is so important. You should ask your instructor if anything is not clear or if there is anything you do not understand.

Always start your judo sessions with warming up exercises. These will prepare your body for the more strenuous exercise of judo and greatly reduce the chance of injury.

I will be pleased to answer any written queries as long as a stamped addressed envelope is enclosed with your letter. You can write to me at 14 Black Dog Walk, Northgate, Crawley, Sussex RH10 2HL.

Have a good time, enjoy your judo, and be safe.

The demonstrations were performed by right-handed judoka. If you are left-handed, change all the rights for lefts and lefts for rights. The easiest way to do this is to use a mirror on the photographs.

MICK LEIGH

About the Contributors

Mick Leigh started Judo in 1955 at the London Judo Society. His first instructor was Ted Cribben, 1st dan and later Kenshiro Abe, 7th dan and Senta Yamada, 6th dan. In 1960 he joined the Renshuden, also in London, where he studied under Trevor Leggett, 7th dan, Saburo Matsushita, 5th dan, and Kisabura Watanabe, 5th dan.

He moved to Sussex in 1964, and in 1965 founded the Mid Sussex Judo Club, which has had many competition successes including men and women in British teams and squads. In 1976 he founded the Kin Ryu Judo Club.

He obtained his 1st dan in 1958, 2nd dan in 1961, 3rd dan in 1966, 4th dan in 1974, 5th dan in 1980, 6th dan in 1986 and 7th dan in 1993. He has represented Great Britain and England was was an Olympic reserve at middleweight in the 1964 Tokyo games. He has been a senior examiner for some years and gained his International Referee's Certificate in 1978. He was an Honorary National Coach of the British Judo Association from 1976 to 1986. In 1979 he was elected to both the BJA Management Committee and the Refereeing Sub-Committee. In 1980 he transferred to the Coaching and Technical Sub-Committee and was made Chairman. He has been a professional coach since 1975 and has been teaching children since 1956. In 1987 he became British Judo Association chairman.

Paul Keevil is a 1st dan. He started judo as a nine-year-old at Croydon and District Judo Society, and practised there until he was 11 years old. He moved to Sussex and stopped his judo for several years, starting again at the Mid Sussex Judo Club with Mick Leigh in 1972. He won the Southern Area Kyu Grade Welterweight Championship at Crystal Palace National Recreation Centre. He has competed in Belgium and Portugal and participated in the Dutch Open and Scandinavian Open Championships. He has represented the Southern Area on several occasions.

Section 1

Chapter 1

The History of Judo

Judo comes from Japan. It is a combat or fighting sport. Judo was founded by a Japanese man named Jigoro Kano. JUDO is composed of two Japanese words, JU meaning 'flexible' or 'supple' and DO meaning 'way'. Judo means, therefore, 'the flexible way'. A person who practises judo is known as a JUDOKA. Jigoro Kano had practised the old Japanese unarmed combat called JIU-JITSU and he decided to make a useful sport out of what was purely a way of fighting without weapons.

He founded the first judo club in 1882 with less than a dozen members. He called his club the Kodokan. The Kodokan is in Tokyo, Japan. Today millions of people all over the world practise judo and the sport is now included in the Olympic Games. At the Munich Olympic Games in 1972, Britain sent a team of six men, and three returned with medals. In the Montreal Olympic Games in 1976, Britain sent a team of five and two returned with medals. No other sport in Britain has been so successful in the Olympic Games (to date).

In the 1980 Moscow Olympics, Neil Adams won a silver medal in the under 71 kg category and Arthur Mapp a bronze in the open. In 1980, in the first Women's World Championships in New York, our ladies proved that they are amongst the best. Jane Bridge (under 48 kg) became Britain's first ever World Champion, and she was not the only success. Dawn Netherwood (under 56 kg) took a silver, and Briggette McCarthy (under 52 kg), Loretta Doyle (under 56 kg) and Avril Malley (under 72 kg) all won bronze medals.

In 1981 Neil Adams (under 78 kg) became our first ever Men's World Champion in Maastricht, Holland.

The second Women's World Championships, held in Paris in 1982 confirmed our place among the leading nations. Loretta Doyle (under 52 kg) and Karen Briggs (under 48 kg) both won gold medals and Diane Bell (under 56 kg) won a bronze.

Our international successes can continue if you practise hard, together with all the other members of your club. Remember fitness, stamina and strength are fairly easy to achieve. Courage can also be developed to a certain extent. Skill is the difficult factor. Many hours have to be spent developing your skill if you have any serious ambition as a competitor.

The first man to beat the Japanese in World Championships and Olympic Games was Anton Geesink, a Dutchman. Now many different countries have taken gold medals in Olympic and World Championships. Japan is having a harder time as judo standards throughout the world are rising, and Great Britain is a major international force in the sport.

Judo was brought to Britain by a Japanese called Gunzi Koizumi. He founded the first Judo Club in Europe, which was situated in London and called the Budokwai. Mr Koizumi died in 1965, but his club remains one of the most successful in the world.

The British Judo Association was formed in 1948. The Association organises judo in Great Britain and selects teams for European, World and Olympic Championships. The British Judo Association is a member of the European Judo Union, and the International Judo Federation. They are usually referred to as the BJA, EJU and IJF.

Because judo comes from Japan, certain customs come with it. Judo's international language is Japanese. All the throws and holds have Japanese names and all refereeing calls are in Japanese. This means that judo people from anywhere in the world can understand each other in judo terminology.

Chapter 2

Dress

The suit worn in judo is called a JUDOGI. There are some rules on how a judogi should fit. For instance, the jacket must cover the thighs. The sleeves must not cover the wrist and be no further than 5 cm (2 inches) up the arm from the wrist. The trousers must not cover the ankle joint and be no further than 5 cm (2 inches) up the knee from the ankle. When the belt is tied there should be about 20 cm (8 inches) hanging from the knot at both ends. The sleeves and trousers should be very loose fitting.

Tying your Trousers

You should always tie your trousers by threading the cord through the loops on the trousers and tying securely with a single knot and a bow.

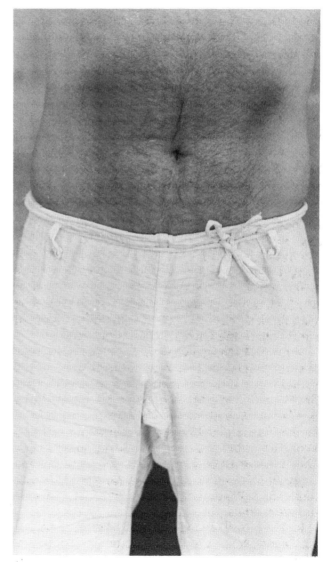

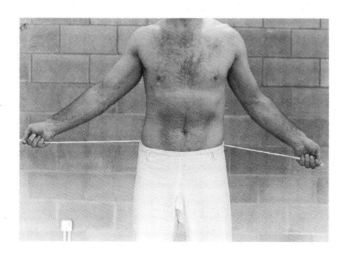

Tying your Belt

1. Wrap the belt around your waist and cross over at the back. The ends should be even in length.
2. Cross the ends over. Drop the top end so that it hangs loose.
3. Tuck the hanging end under the first loop.
4. Tie a square knot.
5. Tighten the knot. The hanging ends should be equal in length.

1

2

3

4

5

Folding and Tying your Judogi

There is a correct way to tie up your judogi if you do not use a holdall or bag. It is a very convenient way because you can then use the loop of belt to carry it over your shoulder.

1. Lay out the jacket as shown in the photograph. Place the trousers inside, folded in half.
2. Bring the lapels in to form a rectangle and fold both sleeves over.
3. Fold both sides into the middle.
4. Fold in half.
5. Double over.
6. Fold the belt in half and tie it round the judogi double so that you finish with a loop. This can be used to hang the judogi over your shoulder.

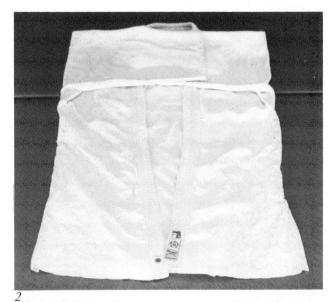

2

1

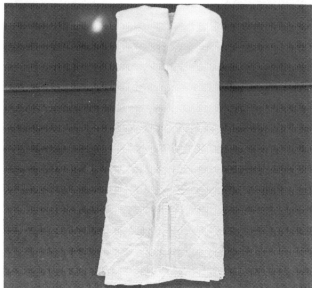

3

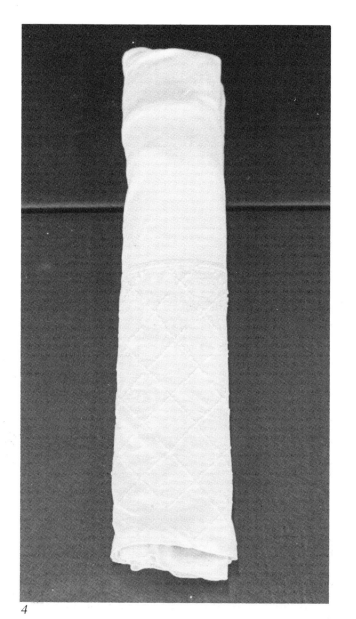

4

5

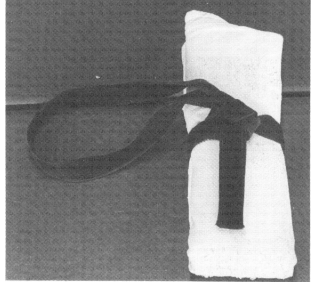

6

Chapter 3

Judo Manners

Safety

As judo is a combat sport it can be dangerous if misused, so remember to follow these few common sense rules for safety.

The DOJO, or judo hall, is the only place for judo demonstration. Never do, or show judo outside a judo club or class. Don't use your skill or strength to bully.

Be careful when you are near the edge of the mat, or TATAMI. You could slip off and land on a spectator. Watch out for other practising pairs, and make sure you don't crash into them.

Don't wear any hard objects, such as rings, earrings, hair clips, necklaces and so on. Keep your finger and toe nails short. Not only can you scratch people, but if your long nails get caught in your partner's costume you can tear your own nails back, which is very painful.

Always obey and respect your instructors.

Never chew gum or sweets on the mat; you may half swallow them and choke. It is wise to take dentures out for the same reason. Never practise with contact lenses in. They are very expensive and easy to lose if they come out.

Always sit or kneel properly and always face the action. You may have to get out of the way quickly.

Avoid talking during practice; you may bite your tongue when bumped or thrown.

Always warm up before practice so that your muscles are ready for action and are not strained by sudden or strenuous movement.

Correct sitting position

Correct kneeling position

Hygiene

This is really a part of safety. If you have verrucae or athlete's foot, do not practise without the permission of your doctor and your instructor.

Never walk on a mat with any sort of footwear, and never walk off a mat without footwear unless you have finished practising. This way the mat is kept clean. A dirty mat is a health hazard as the germs can get into your body if your skin is grazed or cut.

Your body must be clean for practice, particularly your feet. Your toe and finger nails should be checked before practice. They should be clean and not too long.

Your clothing should also be clean so make sure that your judo suit is regularly laundered.

Etiquette

This is a matter of judo manners. Some parts of etiquette were originally used because they involve safety. Sitting or kneeling properly is an example.

Remember we bow in judo because it is a Japanese custom and judo comes from Japan. The word for bow is REI. Whenever you bow you must always make sure your judo suit is tidy and your belt tied up properly.

You should do a standing bow when you walk onto your judo mat, and when you leave. You should also do a standing bow to your partner before and after your practice; also to your opponent, before and after your contest.

It is normal for a class to kneel on one side of the mat and the instructor on the other, facing the class, at the beginning and end of each lesson, for a kneeling bow. All bowing is a matter of courtesy or respect.

Standing bow

Kneeling bow

Chapter 4

Introducing Judo

The Three Parts of Judo

In judo, you are classified as a junior until your sixteenth birthday. You then become a senior. The main difference is that seniors are allowed to do necklocks and armlocks in contests; juniors are not. Please note that this rule could change. In a judo contest your aim is to beat your opponent in one of two ways:

1. Throw them cleanly on their backs with impetus.
2. Hold them down on their back, with you on top, controlling them for 30 seconds. (You cannot hold someone down if you are between their legs. You must first escape from their legs and then hold them down.)

In both these cases, a full point is scored, and the contest won. Lesser scores are possible. For instance, a throw onto the back without sufficient impetus would be scored as a 'near point'. Two of these would equal a full point and win the contest. For this reason most people refer to a near point as a half point. A near point would be scored for a hold down from 25 and less than 30 seconds. Even smaller scores are possible, but your instructor will tell you about them when he (or she) considers you are ready. In all contests the referee uses Japanese calls to control the competitors. The most important of these words are listed on pages 27-33.

The word for contest is SHIAI (shee-eye). There is a winner and a loser. There is a time limit, and control is by a referee.

Contests are only one part of judo. The practice you normally have on club nights is called RANDORI (ran-door-ee). This is not a contest. You and your partner should use randori to improve your judo movements. You must try not to have stiff arms or crouch too much. Try as many throws as possible and move around the mat freely. Try to develop throws on your left side (or your right side if you are left sided). Practise hold downs from both sides, and practise going straight from throws into hold downs. If you are much better or stronger than your partner, you should handicap yourself, for instance by only trying left-side throws, or only throws of a certain type.

There is a third method of judo training called KATA (karter). In kata, one person is always the attacker, and one the defender, or loser. The sequence of movements is fixed and the person being attacked does not resist, but gives the attacker the perfect chance for each technique. If practised often, and properly, you will soon be able to 'feel' the perfect chance when it comes in free practice or contest. You will be better able to take advantage of any chances your opponent gives you if you are trained in kata.

Gradings

When you do judo your skill and knowledge of the sport are shown by the colour of your belt and by the tabs on one end. There are 18 junior grades which are called MONS. Mon means 'gateway', and the word is used because you are entering judo through the gateway of the junior grading system.

Seniors have a different grading system. There are six KYU or 'learner' grades and ten DAN or 'teacher' grades.

Junior Grades

There are six belt colours in the junior grades, from red to brown. Mons are denoted by the tabs on the belt. The following grades are in the process of being confirmed.

Tabs are only necessary on one end of the belt. The tab should go right round the belt. Tabs are 12 mm (½ inch) apart and 12 mm (½ inch) wide. They should be ribbon or tape and sewn on. Ink or sticky tape is not correct.

1st Mon	Red belt with one white tab
2nd Mon	Red belt with two white tabs
3rd Mon	Red belt with three white tabs
4th Mon	Yellow belt with one red tab
5th Mon	Yellow belt with two red tabs
6th Mon	Yellow belt with three red tabs
7th Mon	Orange belt with one red tab
8th Mon	Orange belt with two red tabs
9th Mon	Orange belt with three red tabs
10th Mon	Green belt with one red tab
11th Mon	Green belt with two red tabs
12th Mon	Green belt with three red tabs
13th Mon	Blue belt with one red tab
14th Mon	Blue belt with two red tabs
15th Mon	Blue belt with three red tabs
16th Mon	Brown belt with one red tab
17th Mon	Brown belt with two red tabs
18th Mon	Brown belt with three red tabs

On your sixteenth birthday, remove the red tabs from your belt. You will then be a provisional senior grade of the same colour belt you have. At the first senior grading you take the examiner will award you whatever grade he/she considers you are worth.

Senior Grades

The senior grades progress from a red belt to a brown belt for the kyu grades, which are numbered in reverse. The following kyu grades are in the process of being confirmed.

6th Kyu   Red Belt
5th Kyu   Yellow Belt
4th Kyu   Orange Belt
3rd Kyu   Green Belt
2nd Kyu   Blue Belt
1st Kyu   Brown Belt

1st Dan ⎫
2nd Dan ⎪
3rd Dan ⎬ Black belt
4th Dan ⎪
5th Dan ⎭

6th Dan ⎫
7th Dan ⎬ Red and white blocks on belt
8th Dan ⎭
9th Dan ⎫ Red belt
10th Dan ⎭

Grip and Posture

This is the most basic way to grip in judo.

The feet should be about the same width apart as your shoulders. You must be relaxed and not stiff. The right hand grip uses the right hand on your opponent's lapel with your left hand on his sleeve under the elbow. If you wish to throw your partner by attacking his left side, reverse this grip.

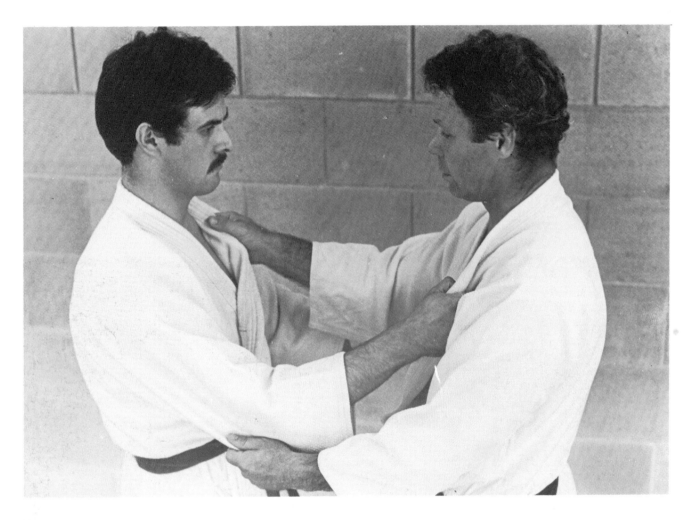

Parts of a Throw

It is possible to divide a throw into three parts for the purpose of study. The first part is the breaking of balance or KUZUSHI (koo-zoo-shee). The second is the fitting of your body into position for the throw, or TSUKURI (soo-koo-ree). Finally, there is the throw itself, or KAKE (kar-kay). This does not mean the throw is done in three parts. The throw is one single continuous movement.

One of the main reasons throws fail is that the thrower fails to break the opponent's balance as he or she attacks. This leaves the opponent on balance and in full control of his or her body. If you come in for the throw (tsukuri) and then try to break balance and throw at the same time, you are not using the correct sequence. Remember – break balance, put your body in position, throw – kuzushi, tsukuri, kake. I again stress that the throw is done in one continuous movement. If you come in for a throw and your partner is off balance, he or she will be momentarily helpless and open to your attack.

Breakfalls

Breakfalls are known as UKEMI (oo-kee-mee). If you are going to move around a lot in randori you will get thrown quite a lot. You need to be able to fall without injury or pain. The most common method of falling safely is to slap the arm on the mat a fraction of a second before your body hits the mat. The arm, therefore, absorbs most of the shock of the fall, thereby preventing any injury. The thrower should help by giving support, usually by holding the sleeve.

The second way to fall painlessly is to roll. This is known as CHUGAERI (shoo-gair-ee). Your body should form as near a circle as possible. Your curved arm is held rigid and is part of the circle. Imagine your body is the rim of a wheel. If you put a wheel or hoop on flat ground it will fall over unless you give it a push. You give your body a push by driving hard off your leading leg. The photographs show two ways of doing a chugaeri or rolling breakfall, one using the other hand to support your weight. Remember to tuck your chin in. Your head must not touch the floor.

Reaping

The word GARI means reaping, and is usually done with the foot or leg. The action is similar to that of a man using a scythe or sickle to cut grass, and you cut your opponent's leg or foot out from under him/her. It is best to take your foot or leg past the point you are reaping and then bring it back. You can only block or pull if you place your leg or foot against your opponent's. In the same way you cannot punch someone if your fist is already in contact with them. You can only push – you need the gap to build up the speed and power. It is the same with the reaping or gari. Take your leg past the point you are going to reap and then bring it back. Ask your instructor to show you the action if you are in any doubt or have any problems.

Chapter 5

Contests

The aim of a contest, or shiai, is to beat your opponent by throwing him cleanly on his back or by holding him down on his back for 30 seconds.

A contest is controlled by a referee. At some contests, such as Area or National Championships, the referee has two judges to help him. They sit on chairs at diagonally opposite corners of the contest area while the referee moves around the area near the contestants.

Contest Rules

The rules of judo are not fixed for ever. They are constantly under review with the intention of improving them wherever possible. The latest contest rules can be obtained from the British Judo Association. Their current address is 7A Rutland Street, Leicester LE1 1RB. They are important for anyone who is interested in competition or championship judo. You may also be able to obtain a copy from your club.

The three most important contest rules are:
1. You must not be passive. You must keep trying to beat your opponent and not just try to stop your opponent beating you.
2. You must both stay in the contest area.
3. You must not do anything against the spirit of judo.

There are also a number of things you must not do in contests, and some of these are listed in the next section.

Some Forbidden Acts During Contests

These are just some of the things you must not do during contests. Your instructor will explain any you do not understand, and tell you more if you are considered ready for them.

Many fouls are not written down in the rules as the list would be too long. These are the common sense things like biting, scratching, kicking, tickling, punching and so on. These fouls are all covered by point number six, 'any act against the spirit of judo'.

1. Pushing on your opponent's face with your hands, feet, arms or legs.

2. Dragging your opponent down for ground work.

3. Leaving the contest area.

4. Forcing your opponent out of the contest area.

5. Performing any act which may endanger your opponent.

6. Performing any act against the spirit of judo.

7. Disregarding the referee's instructions.

8. Holding inside your opponent's sleeve or trouser leg.

9. Holding the same side of your opponent's jacket with both hands for more than five seconds (whilst standing).

10. Holding your opponent's belt for more than five seconds (whilst standing).

11. Continually refusing to take hold of your opponent.

12. Adopting an excessively defensive posture (crouching).

13. Being passive (20-30 seconds standing, with no attack, or 5 seconds standing with both feet completely in the red area and no attack).

14. Continually interlocking your fingers with your opponent's fingers.

NOTE: Passivity will be penalised by shido. Passivity does not apply in the groundwork.

Basic Contest Words and Referee Signals

All the referee's calls in a contest are in Japanese, so you must learn the correct words and signals which he will use.

Word	Meaning	Referee's signal
HAJIME	Begin	No referee signal
SOREMADE	That is all	No referee signal
IPPON	Full point	Referee's arm straight up, palm forward.

| KOKA | Score near yuko | Referee's palm held up | MATTE | Stop | Referee's palm held towards timekeeper |

| PASSIVITY | You must keep up a series of attacks | The hands are rotated around each other | OSAEKOMI | Holding | Referee's arm forward, palm down |

TOKETA   Holding broken   Referee's arm
                                  waved from side
                                  to side

TOKETA   Holding broken   Referee's arm
                                  waved from side
                                  to side

WAZA-ARI   Near point   Referee's arm out   YUKO   Near waza-ari   Referee's arm
to the side   at 45°

SONOMAMA	Do not move	Referee's palms on competitors	HIKI-WAKE	Draw	Arm taken from Ippon position with palm sideways, and brought down with a cutting motion
YOSHI	Carry on	Hands on competitors lifted with call			

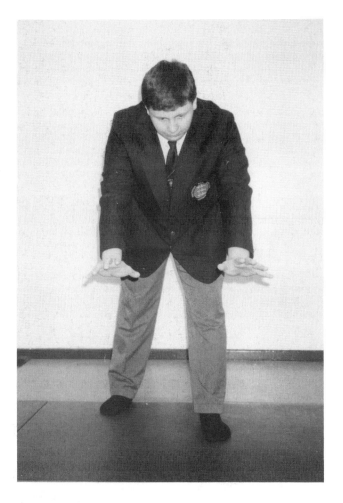

TIDY UP

HANTEI   Referee asking judges for
             decision on winner

Chapter 6

Throws

Do not try any of the following throws until your instructor says you may. He will explain to you the best opportunities to successfully attack for the throws shown.

All the throws are explained and illustrated right-handed. If you are left-handed, change all the rights for lefts, and all the lefts for rights. An easy way to do this is to use a mirror to look at the pictures.

Tai-Otoshi

(Tie-oh-toshee)

Body Drop

Jump in or step round, so you face nearly the same way as your partner (1). Your legs should be spread and your lower rear right leg should be placed against the lower front of your partner's shin. Your left hand pulls round and your right hand drives up and over your right leg. Your right elbow should be down and your fist up. There is no hip or body contact. As you start moving into position you must bring your partner onto the toes of the leg you are attacking. Using your arms, drive your partner over your leg (2).

1

2

O-Soto-Gari

(Oh-soe-toe-gar-ee)

Major Outer Reaping

Step or jump forward with your left foot so it is a few centimetres to the side of your partner's right foot.

Your foot should form a straight line with your partner's two feet (1). Bring your right foot through the gap and into the air behind your partner (2). Point your toes and reap backwards against the back of your partner's upper leg. Don't put your foot on the ground, but swing it through and up into the air. As your leg reaps and swings upwards, your head should go down (3). When you move in for the throw turn your head away from your partner. Try to prop your partner onto the heel of the leg you are reaping.

1

2

Ko-Uchi-Gari

(Koe-oochee-gar-ee)

Minor Inner Reaping

Draw your partner round to your left side, using his or her sleeve to pull on. As your partner steps forward with his or her right foot, slip your right leg between your partner's feet and reap back with the sole of your foot against the back of your partner's right heel (1). As you reap the foot, pull down with the hand holding the sleeve. Your right hip should be close in to your partner's stomach (2).

3

1

O-Uchi-Gari

(Oh-oochee-gar-ee)

Major Inner Reaping

Draw your partner round to your right side, using his or her lapel. As your partner steps round, slip your right leg between your partner's legs and reap back against his/her left leg. As you reap, pull down with the hand holding the lapel. Your foot should reap right round until it is behind you. Your right hip should be close in to your partner's stomach (below).

O-Goshi

(Oh-gosh-ee)

Major Hip

You must move in and turn so you are facing the same way as your partner. Your feet should be nearly together, in front of your partner's feet and pointing in the same direction as his or hers. Your knees must be bent. As you move in your right hand lets go and slips round your partner's waist. Pin your partner to you with your arms (1). Your hip must be pushed through past your partner's hip. Pull strongly with your left hand, straighten your legs and wheel your partner over your hip. Turn your face to your left (2).

1

2

Ippon Seoi-Nage

(Ippon-see-oh-ee-nag-ay)

Single Arm Shoulder Throw

Entry is as for o-goshi, but your hips must be square with your partner's hips. The right arm is driven under your partner's right armpit (1). Your knees must be deeply bent. Pin your partner to you. To throw, snap your hips back and up and take your head forward and down (2).

1

2

Ko-Soto-Gari

(Koe-soe-toe-gar-ee)

Minor Outer Reaping

Move round to your partner's right side, so you face his hip (1). Reap the right heel with the sole of your left food in the direction your partner's toes are pointing (2). Pull down towards the ground with your left hand as you reap. As you move in try and take your partner onto the heel that you are attacking.

1

2

Tsuri-Komi-Goshi

(Sooree-komm-ee-gosh-ee)

Lifting Drawing Hip

Move in and turn so you are facing the same way as your partner. Your feet should be under your hips and in front of your partner's and pointing the same way. As you move in, use your arms to tilt your partner onto the toes of both feet (1). Your knees are bent and your hip pushed past your partner's hip. Your right elbow must be down and your fist up. Pin your partner to you. Straighten your knees and lift and pull your partner over your hip (2).

1

2

Chapter 7

Hold Downs

Do not try any of the following hold downs until your instructor says you can.

All the hold downs are explained and illustrated right-handed. If you are left-handed, change all the rights for lefts, and all the lefts for rights.

If you are in pain at any time and wish to submit or 'give in', tap your partner twice or more, or bang the mat twice or more with your arm or leg, or call out 'yes'. Always let go if someone submits.

Hon-Kesa-Gatame

(Hon-Kez-er-gat-armay)

Basic Scarf Holding

1. Your hip must be in contact with your partner's side.

2. Your hips and head must be as low as possible.

3. Your partner's arm must be tightly trapped.

4. Your legs must be spread and the front leg should have the little toe on the ground.

Hon-Yoko-Shiho-Gatame

(Hon-yoe-ko-shee-hoe-gatarmay)

Basic Side Four Quarters

1. Your chest weight must be on your partner's chest.

2. One knee should be tightly against your partner's hip and your other leg straight, with the toes tucked under and the knee on the ground.

3. Your hips must be as low as possible.

4. Turn your face towards your partner's face and keep your chin in.

Hon-Kami-Shiho-Gatame

(Hon-kammee-shee-hoe-gatarmay)

Basic Upper Four Quarters

1. Your chest weight must be on your partner's chest.

2. Your hips must be as low as possible.

3. Your arms go under your partner's shoulders and grip the belt.

4. Your legs wide apart, toes tucked under, knees on the ground.

5. One side of your face should be on your partner's stomach, with your chin in.

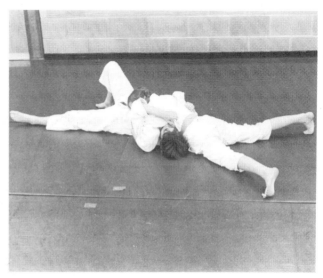

Hon-Tate-Shiho-Gatame

(Hon-tar-tay-shee-hoe-gatarmay)

Basic Lengthwise Four Quarters

1. Sit astride your partner's stomach and entwine your legs by taking them outwards and under your partner's. Lie along your partner's chest.

2. Trap an arm and wrap your right arm round your partner's neck. Grip the cloth with both hands. Your left hand holds your own right collar.

3. Keep your hips as low as possible.

4. Keep your forehead near the mat.

5. There are many variations of this hold.

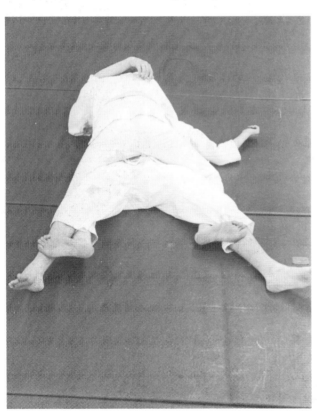

Kata-Gatame

(Karter-gatarmay)

Shoulder Holding

This hold down is very similar to kesa-gatame. The difference is in the trapping of your partner's arm. Instead of trapping it under your armpit, place it by your partner's right ear and trap it there with your head. Link your hands together in the 'butcher's hook' grip. Remember this can be a painful hold so don't squeeze too hard to start with. Just strongly enough to control is sufficient. Other major points are the same as kesa-gatame. There is another way to do kata-gatame. Ask your instructor to show you.

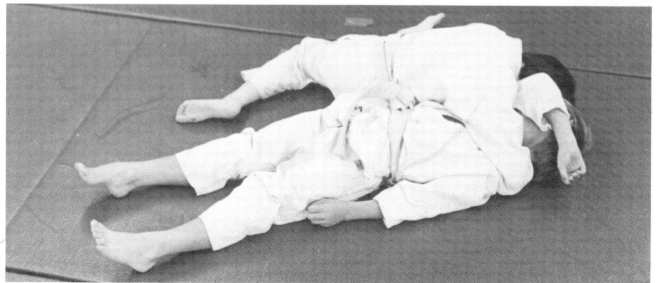

Mune-Gatame

(Moon-ee-gatarmay)

Chest Holding

1. This hold down is similar to yoko-shiho-gatame. Your chest weight must be on your partner's chest.

2. Keep your hips as low as possible.

3. One knee should be in at the hip and the other out straight, with the toes under.

4. The major difference between mune-gatame and yoko-shiho-gatame is in the use of your arms. Wrap them both round your partner's shoulder and grip the cloth.

Questionnaire

If you have read this book carefully, you should know the answers to all these questions.

1. What does 'judo' mean?

2. How many junior grades are there?

3. What do these words mean? (a) ukemi (b) judoka (c) judogi (d) dojo (e) tatami

4. How do you submit if you are in pain?

5. What country does judo come from?

6. Why do we bow?

7. What does 'mon' mean?

8. At what age do you become a senior?

9. What is your instructor's name?

10. What is your club called?

11. Why shouldn't you chew sweets or gum on the mat?

12. How many throws can you name?

13. How many hold downs can you name?

14. What do these words mean? hajime (b) soremade (c) ippon (d) waza-ari (e) matte (f) toketa (g) osaekomi.

15. Who founded judo?

16. Who brought judo to Britain?

17. Why is it important to have short finger and toe nails?

18. Do you know three things you must not do in contests?

19. Can you tie your belt and trousers properly?

20. What grade is a yellow belt with two red tabs?

21. Why should you warm up before practice?

22. What association does your club belong to?

23. How do you score an ippon?

24. How do you score a waza-ari?

25. Why should you sit or kneel properly?

26. Why should you not talk during practice?

27. What is a judo suit called?

28. What does rei mean?

29. What was the first judo club called?

30. Who was the first non-Japanese to win a World Judo title? What nationality was he?

31. What do these initials stand for? (a) BJA (b) BJC (c) EJU (d) IJF.

32. What is kata-gatame?

33. What is o-goshi?

34. What signal does the referee make for ippon?

35. What signal does the referee make for waza-ari?

36. Where is the British Judo Association Headquarters?

37. Which two types of groundwork techniques are not allowed for juniors?

38. What is the person who grades you called?

39. What is the youngest age you can be graded?

40. What does 'tsukuri' mean?

Section 2

Chapter 8

Judo Contests

In any judo contest, or shiai, your aim is to beat your opponent either by throwing them cleanly on their backs with impetus; or by holding them down on their backs, with you on top, for 30 seconds. If you do not beat your opponent in either of these ways, you can gain other lesser scores.

Contest Scores

In the first section, I explained that scoring an IPPON, or full point, would end a contest. An ippon is scored by either throwing your opponent onto his back with impetus, or holding him on his back with you controlling him for 30 seconds.

If you throw him onto his back without enough impetus, or hold him down for 25 but less than 30 seconds, you score a WAZA-ARI or near point. Two waza-aris equal one ippon, and finish the contest. When a second waza-ari is scored by the same person, the referee makes the waza-ari signal and then the ippon signal, calling WAZA-ARI AWASETE (a-wa-set-ay) IPPON, SOREMADE, which means near point, two near points make one point, that is all.

You can score two waza-aris with hold downs, or with throws, or one with a throw and one with a hold down.

If you throw your opponent onto his side, you score a YUKO (yoo-koe), near waza-ari. If you hold your opponent on his back for 20 but less than 25 seconds, you also score a yuko. However many yukos you score, they never add up to a higher score. One waza-ari will beat any number of yukos.

If you throw your opponent onto his buttocks or hip, you score a KOKA (koe-ka) near yuko. If you hold down your opponent for 10 seconds but less than 20 seconds, you score a koka. However many kokas you score they will never add up to a higher score. One yuko will beat any number of kokas.

The two smallest scores are not called or signalled. The referee and judges keep a mental tally. A KINSA is a superior attack. If your opponent twists out of a throw and lands on his stomach you score a kinsa. If you get a considerable result from a throw, for instance he has to fall on his knee or put an arm or elbow down as the result of a **good** attack you score a kinsa. A hold down that is called and escaped from in less than 10 seconds is a kinsa. Any number of kinsas are beaten by any called score.

If you get a definite reaction from a **good** attack you will be credited with an attack. If you have your opponent in serious risk of a hold down but he just managed to avoid it you will be credited with an attack. You must be careful to make genuine attacks. Just "flopping" or "dropping" with no intent of throwing should be penalised a SHIDO for a false attack.

If there are no scores on the board at the end of the contest or the scores are equal, the referee will award the contest to the person with the most kinsas. If there is no difference in the number of kinsas each, the referee will award the contest to the person making the most attacks and he will win.

Boys' Weight Categories

Up to and including 31 kg
Over 31 kg and up to and including 34 kg
Over 34 kg and up to and including 37 kg
Over 37 kg and up to and including 41 kg
Over 41 kg and up to and including 45 kg
Over 45 kg and up to and including 50 kg
Over 50 kg and up to and including 55 kg
Over 55 kg and up to and including 60 kg
Over 60 kg and up to and including 65 kg
Over 65 kg and up to and including 71 kg
Over 71 kg

Girls' Weight Categories

Up to and including 30 kg
Over 30 kg and up to and including 33 kg
Over 33 kg and up to and including 36 kg
Over 36 kg and up to and including 40 kg
Over 40 kg and up to and including 44 kg
Over 44 kg and up to and including 48 kg
Over 48 kg and up to and including 52 kg
Over 52 kg and up to and including 56 kg
Over 56 kg and up to and including 61 kg
Over 61 kg and up to and including 66 kg
Over 66 kg

These weights are not necessarily permanent and may be changed. Check with your coach. These are national weights. At area and below lower weight categories (and also different categories) are sometimes used.

Pools Competitions

Judo competitions can be run in several different ways. One way is to organise competitors into pools. For convenience, we will assume there are 32 competitors. They could be split into eight pools, or groups, of four. Each person in each group would fight everyone in their group. Every competitor would therefore have three contests. The top two in each pool would go through into the next round which would consist of four pools of four. If the top two from each of these groups went through, there would be eight competitors left. These could fight in a further two pools or have quarter finals, semi finals and finals.

Knockout Competitions

For a knockout competition, the 32 competitors would be split into two groups, A and B. The competitors would be paired up for eight contests in each group, and the winners would go on to fight each other in four contests and so on, each group running a straight knockout until there was a winner from each group. These two would be the finalists, fighting for the gold and silver medals.

Repêchage Competitions

A repêchage competition is similar to a knockout competition in the first stages, one competitor winning through to the final from each of two knockout groups.

If you fight in a repêchage competition and get beaten, however, you still have a chance of a bronze medal unless the competitor who beat you loses before reaching the final.

As soon as the competitor has won the group and goes through to the final, you will have your chance to fight through for a bronze medal in the repêchage. If you are beaten a second time, then you are eliminated.

Contest Words

In the first section, I explained the basic contest words and the most common referee signals. You are now ready to learn the additional words and signals in the next two sections.

Word	Meaning
KOKA	Near yuko
YUKO	Near waza-ari
SHIDO	Note
CHUI	Caution
KEIKOKU	Warning or reprimand
HANSOKU	Disqualification
GACHI	Win
MAKE	Loss
HIKEWAKE	Draw
HANTEI	Request for judges' decision on winner
YUSEI GACHI	Superiority win
WAZA-ARI-AWASETE-IPPON	Near point – two equal a full point

Basic Contest Tactics

One of the most important rules in judo is that you must not leave the contest area. Even stepping out with one foot is considered to be leaving the contest area. It does not matter whether you mean to or not. So do not let your opponent push you until you are on the edge of the mat with your back to the edge. It is even worse if you are forced into one of the corners. If your opponent is pushing you, do not push back, just move round in a circle, so you are facing the edge of the mat. Remember it is an offence to push your opponent out – the problem the referee has to decide is who is to blame. Therefore, if you never allow yourself to be pushed out and you never try to push your opponent out, you will never be penalised for it. A list of the penalties is on page 58.

You must keep up a regular series of attacks, or you may be penalised for passivity. If you are guilty of passivity, the referee will stop the contest and give you the passivity signal, (see page 29). You will be penalised a shido, then a chui, and so on until you are disqualified. It is therefore important to practise constantly attacking in randori otherwise you will become tired before the end of the contest.

Do not be predictable. Your opponent should never know what you are going to do next. You must vary the speeds with which you move, the way in which you move and also the ways you grip.

Some throws have special ways of holding. The very fact that you hold in a certain way can give your throw away before you try it. If you just settle into one grip, your opponent will know that he only has a limited number of attacks to contend with. This leaves him freer to attack you. If you change your grip and sometimes attack on a different side, your opponent will have to spread his defences and will be less able to tell which way to defend next.

If you throw your opponent, never assume that you have scored an ippon. Always follow up your advantage immediately with a hold down. If you have scored ippon, all well and good, but if you have scored less, then at least you have the chance of completing your victory on the ground. In the event of your opponent being close to the edge of the contest area, pull him or her back into the area, and then hold them down. Ask your instructor to show you how to do this. If you have a hold on the edge, and during the struggle you both leave the contest area, the referee will call 'matte' (stop). This means that you will lose your hold down and start again from the standing position.

If your opponent is on all fours, always attack from the side or rear if possible. If you go to the head end, you will find your legs can be grabbed and you may be capsized and held down (see page 62).

Never let your opponent get his legs around your legs or body. If they do you must escape (see page 64).

Renrakuwaza

Very often an opponent will have a good defence against your throws. This is the time to use combination techniques or renrakuwaza (ren-rak-oo-wazza).

A very popular combination is tai-otoshi and o-uchi-gari. If you attack with tai-otoshi, your opponent will very often step over your leg. Your leg would immediately reap back against your opponent's left leg (if you have attacked right-handed). Then throw with o-uchi-gari. It also works in reverse. Try o-uchi-gari, and your opponent will very often lift the attacked leg to evade your reap. Switch your attacking leg straight across, pivot to your left, and block the front of your opponent's right leg and throw with tai-otoshi. Ask your coach to show you.

There are many ways to combine different throws. Try to find some and ask your coach to help you.

Sportsmanship

You are a judoka. A high standard of sportsmanship is expected of you. This will sometimes mean you have to use a great deal of self-control or self-discipline. A bad sportsperson is generally disliked and no-one wants to be disliked. If you get a decision against you, that is just bad luck. If you do judo for any length of time, you will get decisions for you when you should have lost. No human being is incapable of error. Referees are human and also make mistakes. They are doing a difficult job to the best of their ability. Many times I have seen people fuss because they thought they should have won, and they did not know the rules properly.

Get a copy of the IJF Rules either from your club or from the BJA at 7A Rutland Street, Leicester LE1 1RB. If you think referees are wrong every time they do not give you the call you want, then try an experiment. Ask your instructor to let you referee some contests at your club, and then let your instructor and club-mates comment on your efforts. You may learn something!

Tomoe-Nage

Penalties

If you infringe judo rules in a contest you will be penalised. Each penalty is equivalent to a score. The first (smallest) penalty is SHIDO. This is used if you have committed some foul that is not dangerous or serious; the second is CHUI. You receive a chui if you repeat a small foul (or already have a shido) or commit a more serious foul. If you commit a further small foul and already have a chui, or if you commit a quite serious foul, you would be penalised KEIKOKU. If you commit a further small foul or commit a very grave infringement, you receive HANSOKU MAKE (disqualification).

Score	Penalty
KOKA (near yuko)	SHIDO (note) (shee-doe)
YUKO (near waza-ari)	CHUI (caution) (choo-ee)
WAZA-ARI (near point)	KEIKOKU (warning) (kay-kok-oo)
IPPON (full point)	HANSOKUMAKE (disqualification) (Han-sok-oo-mak-ay)

Penalties are transferred as the score. Therefore, if you have been penalised shido your opponent will be credited with koka.

Scores

Any number of kokas will be beaten by one yuko. Any number of yukos will be beaten by one waza-ari. A second waza-ari will equal ippon and finish the contest.

Penalties

No penalty will be given twice. The referee has to give at least one penalty higher. The previous penalty is removed from the scoreboard.

Referee's Superiority Decisions

Referee's superiority decisions are based on the number of attacks and kinsas during the contest. They are known as YUSEI-GACHI. Here are some examples of these referee decisions:

Red	White
2 kokas	1 koka
1 shido	

Referee's decision on kinsas and attacks

Red	White
1 waza-ari	1 koka
1 keikoku	

White wins

Red	White
1 yuko	3 yukos
1 chui	1 shido
1 koka	

White wins

Further Prohibited Acts

1. Diving into the mat head first whilst trying a throw such as harai-goshi or hane-goshi, brings disqualification (hansokumake).

2. To intentionally disarrange your judogi or to tie or untie your belt or trousers without the referee's permission (shido).

3. To take hold of your opponent's foot or leg unless simultaneously attacking.

4. To wind the end of the belt or jacket round any part of the opponent's body more than 360 degrees (shido).

5. Kicking with your knee or foot your opponent's hand or arm to make him or her release a grip (chui).

6. To lift someone who is on their back off the ground in order to drive them back into the mat (keikoku).

7. Sweeping your opponent's supporting leg from the inside when he or she is trying a technique such as harai-goshi (keikoku). See photographs right.

8. Making unnecessary calls or gestures derogatory to your opponent during the contest (keikoku).

9. To intentionally fall back onto someone who is clinging to your back (hansokumake).

This is allowed.

This is not allowed.

Chapter 9

Grouping of Techniques

There are a large number of techniques in judo. They have been formed into groups for simplicity and easy reference.

Groundwork

Groundwork is known as KATAME-WAZA (kat-am-ay-wazza), or sometimes NE-WAZA (nay-wazza). These are the main divisions.

1. Hold downs   OSAEKOMI-WAZA (oh-sye-kommee-wazza)

2. Joint locks   KANSETSU-WAZA (kan-setsoo-wazza)

3. Neck locks   SHIME-WAZA (shim-ay-wazza)

Throws

These are known as TACHI-WAZA (tach-ee-wazza). They can be sub-divided as follows.

1. Hand and shoulder throws   TE-WAZA (tay-wazza)

2. Hip throws   KOSHI-WAZA (kosh-ee-wazza)

3. Foot and leg throws   ASHI-WAZA (ash-ee-wazza)

4. Rear body sacrifice throws   MA-SUTEMI-WAZA (mar-sutemee-wazza)

5. Side body sacrifice throws   YOKO-SUTEMI-WAZA (yoe-koe-sutemee-wazza)

A sacrifice throw is one where you fall to the ground in order to throw your opponent.

Chapter 10

Some Groundwork Techniques

For all the groundwork activities illustrated on the following pages, reverse 'right' for 'left' if you are escaping from the opposite side from the one illustrated.

Turning Over Opponent on All Fours

Method 1: Further Arm

Kneel by your opponent's side facing him or her. Reach under his/her chest and hook your hand round the further arm. Reach under his/her face and hook your hand over your other hand. Push strongly with your shoulder and chest, and pull with your arms. Your opponent should be forced over onto their back. Don't interlock your fingers.

Method 2: Quarter Nelson

Kneel by your opponent's side facing him/her. Place the hand nearest your opponent's head onto his/her head. Your other arm is threaded under your opponent's nearest armpit and your hand placed on your arm just above the wrist. Lever your opponent over by pulling in towards your knees. Do not force your opponent's head straight down as this endangers the spine.

Escape From Between the Legs

Method 1: Over the Leg

1. Hold your opponent's belt with your left hand.

2. Press on the inside of your opponent's left knee with your right hand – push the leg down to mat.

3. Slip your right knee over your opponent's leg, leaving your foot behind as a bridge.

4. 'Escape' your left leg.

5. Take your right foot out and secure holding.

2

1

3

4

5

Method 2: Under the Leg

1. Hold your opponent's belt with your left hand.

2. Your right arm is placed under your opponent's left leg.

3. Lift your opponent's leg onto your right shoulder.

4. Reach across your opponent's chest with your right arm and take hold of his/her right lapel (keep the arm bent).

5. Slip out from under your opponent's leg and secure holding.

1

2

4

3

5

Single Arm Roll

1. You are on all fours: your opponent is attacking you from the side and has reached over your back and under your chest or armpit with his/her right arm.

2. Reach up and back with your arm, trapping the attacker's arm above the elbow.

3. Bring your arm under your body to thoroughly secure the attacker's arm.

4/5. Bring your furthest knee in towards the attacker and roll the attacker over your back, finally securing a holding.

2

1

3

Double Arm Roll

4

5

1. You are on all fours: your opponent is attacking from your head end. He/she wraps both arms around your chest.

2. You reach up and back with both arms in order to trap your opponent's arms above the elbows.

3. Bring your arms under your body to thoroughly secure the attacker's arms and form a butcher's hook with your hands.

4. Roll, either to the right or left, and as your opponent is rolled over, spread your legs wide. You now have a hold down.

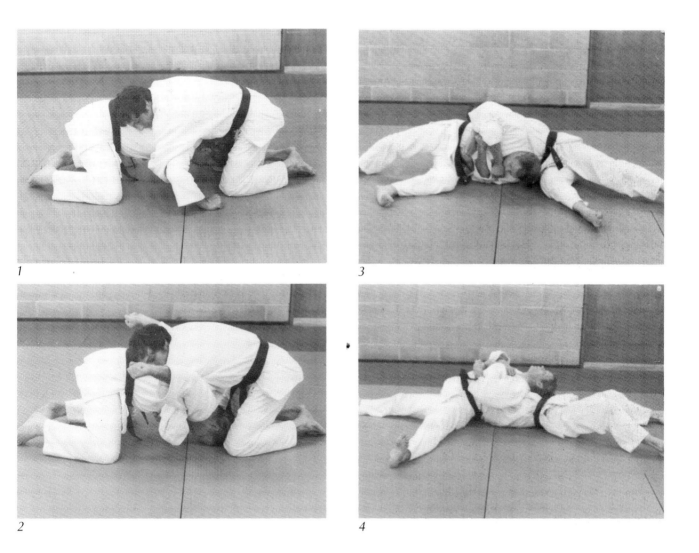

1

2

3

4

Chapter 11

Throws

All these throws are explained and illustrated right-handed. If you are left-handed, use a mirror to change all the rights for lefts, and all the lefts for rights.

De-Ashi-Harai

or De-Ashi-Harai (Dee-ashee-ha-rye)

Your opponent has the right foot in front of the left and is moving the foot (either forward or backward).

Before the weight is placed on the foot, you sweep with your left sole against the outside of your opponent's foot.

As you sweep with your foot, your hands take your opponent in the direction of the throw. Use them as if you are steering a car to the left. Your sweeping leg must be straight and must follow your opponent's leg up.

This throw is also called de-ashi-barai.

2

3

Hiza-Guruma

(Hiz-a-gurooma)

Your opponent has stepped forward with the left foot. You pivot your right foot to point towards your opponent's right foot and place the sole of your left foot against his/her leg slightly below and on the outside of the knee.

Pull outwards and upwards with your left hand (towards your left) and upwards and over in the direction of the throw with your right hand.

Continue the pull and push with your hands and withdraw your left hip and shoulder.

Your blocking leg must be straight. Keep foot contact on your opponent's leg as long as possible.

2

1

3

Sasae-Tsuri-Komi-Ashi

(Sas-ay-sooree-kommi-ashee)

Tilt your opponent onto the toes of his/her right foot. Step out to your right with your right foot, turning the toes in. Place the sole of your left foot against the front of your opponent's lower shin.

Lift upwards and outwards with your left hand and up and round with your right hand.

As your opponent loses his/her balance and starts falling, continue to press the sole of the foot against his/her shin.

2

1

3

Uki-Goshi

(Ookee-goshee)

Draw opponent up onto his/her toes and step forward with your right foot. As you do so, encircle your opponent's waist with your right arm and take your left leg back.

Clamp your opponent to you with both arms. Your right hip should be tight against your opponent's right hip.

2

1

3

Twist your hips in an anti-clockwise direction parallel to the ground. Your opponent should be thrown round your hip and not over your hip as in o-goshi. Turn your head to the left.

Harai-Goshi

(Ha-rye-goshee)

As your opponent puts the weight onto his/her right foot, tilt them up onto the toes (of the right foot), spin in and clamp your opponent to you. Your right leg goes forward and into the air, toes pointing.

Your left hand pulls up and across your chest and the right hand lifts your opponent. They should be stretched up onto the toes of the leg you are sweeping.

2

1

3

Sweep back and up with the right leg. As the leg goes up, the head goes down. The toes of the sweeping foot should be higher than your head.

Hane-Goshi

(Ha-nay-goshee)

Your opponent is momentarily facing you square. Draw him/her onto the toes as you jump in and turn.

Your right leg is bent and placed down the front of your opponent's right leg. Your little toe is in contact with your opponent's shin. You must not bend forward at the hips.

Spring your opponent up on your leg, hip and trunk. Your body should form a straight line, from right toes to head. Turn out to the left and complete the throw.

1

2

Tomoe-Nage

(Toe-moe-ay-na-gay)

Ideally, you should hold both lapels, but this is sometimes a giveaway. You have to decide on either the ideal grip or the advantage of surprise.

Your opponent pushes you. Swing under him/her, placing the sole of your right foot diagonally in the pit of your opponent's stomach.

Your left leg should be well through your opponent's legs. Push with the foot and pull with the hands.

The main danger with this throw (and sumi-gaeshi) is if it fails you may get held down.

2

1

3

Your opponent's body should move in a large arc over your body. Be prepared to follow through for groundwork. Ask your coach how to do this.

Sumi-Gaeshi

(Soo-mee-gay-shee)

This is a good throw to use against someone who crouches.

Your opponent has his/her left foot forward. Enter by swinging under. Your right foot is hooked in behind your opponent's left knee. Your left foot is well through your opponent's legs.

Pull your opponent over by hands and foot, so he/she describes an arc over your body.

They should fall to your left corner, behind your head. Be prepared to follow through with groundwork.

2

1

3

Chapter 12

Hold Downs

The hold downs are also explained and illustrated right-handed.

Do not forget that if you are in pain at any time and wish to submit, tap your partner twice or more, or bang the mat twice or more with your arm or leg, or call out 'yes'. Always let go if someone submits.

Makura-Kesa-Gatame

(Mak-oora-kezza-gat-arm-ay)

Sit by your opponent's right ear, facing his/her head end. Spread your legs as for kesa-gatame. Your right hand goes under your opponent's left armpit. Your opponent's head rests on your right upper leg. Your right hand hooks over your right leg. Hold your opponent's collar with your left hand.

Keep your left foot well back as you may be weak in that direction. Keep your head down.

Ushiro-Kesa-Gatame

(Ooshee-roe-kessa-gat-arm-ay)

Sit by your opponents left ear, facing his/her feet. Lean across the chest and hold the belt. Trap his/her left arm under your left armpit and hold the sleeve.

Keep your head down on the chest. Your legs are as for kesa-gatame.

Kuzure-Kesa-Gatame

(K'z-ooree-keza-gat-arm-ay)

As kesa-gatame but your right arm goes under the left armpit of your opponent. You can have your right hand on the mat or hold onto your opponent's collar. You should sit higher than kesa-gatame.

Kuzure-Yoko-Shiho-Gatame

(K'z-ooree-yoe-koe-shee-hoe-gat-arm-ay)

As yoko-shiho-gatame but your left arm goes under your opponent's left shoulder instead of round his/her neck.

Kuzure-Kami-Shiho-Gatame

(K'z-ooree-kammi-shee-hoe-gat-arm-ay)

As kami-shiho-gatame but one of your opponent's arms is trapped under your armpit and with the hand on that side you hold under your opponent's collar.

Lie on the side of the shoulder you have trapped.

Chapter 13

Armlocks and Necklocks

Since 1 January 1980, armlocks (KANSETSU-WAZA) and necklocks (SHIME-WAZA) have been allowed in some junior contests for boys over 55 kg and girls over 52 kg.

Do not do any armlocks or necklocks unless your instructor gives you permission. Make sure you both understand the submission signals. Never jerk when you apply an armlock or necklock. Always release the hold immediately your partner submits.

Juji-Gatame

This is a common armlock. A lock can only be put on the elbow joint.

Okuri-Eri-Jime

This is a common necklock.

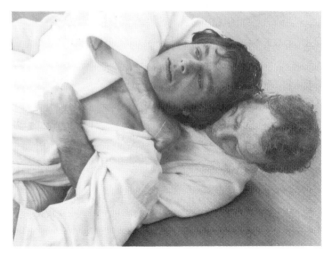

Section 2

Questionnaire

1. How many groups of throws are there?
2. How many groups of groundwork techniques are there?
3. What is the word for groundwork?
4. What is the word for standing judo?
5. What are te-waza?
6. What are kansetsu-waza?
7. What is a (a) koka   (b) yuko?
8. What is the referee's signal for passivity?
9. What score is chui equal to?
10. What penalty is waza-ari equal to?
11. What does waza-ari awesete ippon mean?
12. How many seconds hold down scores yuko?
13. You have two kokas and a shido against you. Your opponent has two kokas. Who wins?
14. How do you score a koka from a throw?
15. How many points do a waza-ari score? And an ippon?
16. What is the difference between pools and repêchage?
17. If you win all your contests in the repêchage, which medal would you get?
18. What is the penalty for stepping out of the contest area?
19. What is the penalty for leaving the contest area during a throw when your body touches out before your opponent's?
20. Which grips are illegal? When are they illegal?
21. What are renrakuwaza?
22. What are the groups of sacrifice throws called?
23. What are the referee's signals for koka and yuko?
24. When was your club founded?
25. Which area is your club in?
26. Who are the current British Men/Women Middleweight Champions?
27. Who are the current British Men/Women Light-weight Champions?
28. What happens to your grade when you become 16 years old?
29. What does kuzuri mean?
30. Classify the throws in this booklet into te-waza, koshi-waza and so on, and check your answers with your instructor.
31. What is the youngest age you can enter official competition?
32. How many boys'/girls' weight categories are there?
33. What is your weight category?
34. How do you score a kinsa?

Section 3

Chapter 14

Developing Your Skills

Acquiring and developing your skills is a time-consuming activity. Judo skills and techniques are not 'just there', they must be developed through understanding and practice.

I am sure you have noticed that most contests are won on the ground. This is because developing a good ippon-scoring throw is no easy matter. It is very tempting to work on your ne-waza at the expense of tachi-waza. This is a mistake. Assume you have eight contests to reach a final. If each one goes to time, or is won after a strength-sapping period of ne-waza, you will reach the final in poor condition for the contest. If your opponent has won most contests by ippon throws early in each contest, he or she will be in much better shape for the final.

When you watch someone with a good ippon-scoring throw, it looks very simple. The truth is that all the work has been done outside the contest period. Without a good throwing technique all the work is done inside the contest period.

The problem is how to develop a good throwing technique. I believe that a sequence of training something like this should be followed.

1. Learn the basic throwing technique 'static'. That means your partner does not move around or try to stop your throw. 'Jumping' is also very unhelpful. This way you can practise the throw in ideal circumstances and be sure that your technique is correct.

2. Move forwards, backwards or sideways in a straight line, and find the right moment for launching your attack. Remember, if you wait for the right moment it will be gone before you can get into position. A marksman aims in front of a moving target. The bullet arrives at the moment the target is at the same point in space.

3. Attempt your throw against a partner moving at random.

4. Attempt the throw while your partner tries to evade, but not block, it.

5. Your partner should finally give you more specific problems to overcome, such as straight arms, crouching and so on.

If you work hard and regularly, you will develop a good throw over a period of time. It will still fail on some occasions, however, and if you develop only a limited number of throws, you will become known for whichever throws you have developed. Ne-waza is still vital, as you will not score ippon every time.

Now is the time to develop a 'lead-in' throw. This should by-pass your opponent's conscious thought and his body should react by reflex. Your lead-in throw should make your opponent react by moving in a specific way, depending on the throw you are developing, in order to put him in a vulnerable position for your major throw.

As an example, take ko-uchi-gari used as a lead-in for ippon-seoi-nage. Your attack should make your opponent take the attacked foot back. This takes your attacking foot into position for your major attempt. You only have to insert the arm and take the other foot back into position. Note also that you do not have to turn a full 180 degrees, if you throw in the right direction. This has the advantage of reducing the time taken for your major attack.

This gives you two alternatives.

1. You can attack directly with your major throw.

2. You can attack with your lead-in first, in order to set up your opponent for your major throw.

Let us assume that your major throwing attack has failed. Think about what your opponent has done to stop your throw. What throw could you use as a lead-out technique to use his defensive move against him? Ask your coach to help you.

You now have three techniques. They should all be strong enough to help you score frequently. But you must never stop working on them. If you score with the first technique you may go into ne-waza if you wish, similarly with the second and third techniques. You should become adept at entering ne-waza via any of these attacks.

Always use your randori time constructively. Mat time is valuable; do not waste it. You can get fit and strong outside the dojo, but judo skills are learnt and developed in practice. Obsession with general fitness at the expense of skill is counter-productive. The two should develop side by side.

Don't contest all the time as this does not help to develop much technical skill. Randori should consist of give and take. If you are good enough to keep throwing your partner, you will soon run short of people willing to take you on in randori. You should both gain from each practice. Tell your partner what you are trying to do and find out what he or she wants to practise. That way you can work as a team and both develop your technique.

Grip Fighting

It is necessary for you to learn how to fight for grips. Often a competitor has a favourite grip for his tokui-waza (best throw). If you can get your best hold and at the same time prevent your opponent getting his, you will have a great advantage. When you move around the contest area, use your whole body to move your opponent and not just your arms. Vary your length of step. This can make your opponent over-reach. Don't move too much in the same direction. Try not to be repetitive in your judo.

Check with your coach on which grips are legal and which are illegal. This is most important. You can use illegal grips in randori as there is no referee to penalise you. In contests you will soon regret not knowing which grips are either not allowed, or have some time limitation.

Lastly, do not take grip fighting to extremes. You must take hold in order to throw.

Chapter 15

Throws

Sode-Tsuri-Komi-Goshi

This throw requires a double-sleeve grip. The grips should be under the sleeve and not over. A great advantage with this throw is that you can attack on the left or right, as you control both sides.

Entry is as for tsuri-komi-goshi, but the right hand drives your partner's left arm up as you make entry. Keep your right elbow and upper arm against your side as you step in with your right foot. This is a great help in breaking a stiff left arm defence as your body and arm will be more powerful than the defender's arm alone.

Drive your partner's left arm over in the direction of your left shoulder. Both of your arms should be drawing your partner onto his toes as your body makes contact. Your right hip is pushed through past your partner's right hip and your arms should be pushing/pulling him into strong contact.

Complete the throw with the face and shoulders turning to the left. The grip on the sleeve you are driving up should be reversed so you can 'punch'. Get your partner moving round and see if he can slip off your hip. If he does try, use his movement to draw him up into a left sode-tsuri-komi-goshi.

This throw can be linked with kata-guruma or ippon-seoi-nage. See if you can find out how to combine them (using sode-tsuri-komi-goshi as your first attack).

1

3

4

Morote-Seoi-Nage

With this throw it is possible to damage your wrist, elbow or shoulder if you fail to break your opponent's balance to the front in your preparation.

Attack (right side) as your opponent steps forward with his left foot. Your arms must be drawing him up onto his toes.

Place your right foot in position and take your left foot back. Your feet must be parallel to your opponent's feet. Your knees should bend as you make

1

2

your entry. Make tight contact between your back and your opponent's front. Your elbow is inserted under your opponent's armpit as you make your entry. Practice is required to get the contact and feet positioned correctly. If your hip goes too far through, your opponent will slip off your left side. If your hip is not through enough he will slip off your right side. A fast, light entry is required and the kuzushi should be just enough to take some weight off his heels.

To complete the throw take the hips back into your opponent and the head down.

Some competitors use this throw with a double lapel grip. If this grip is used, uke must be turned over quickly so that he cannot block the throw by placing a hand on the ground. This is not a recommended escape but sometimes is a reflex action on the part of the defender.

4

3

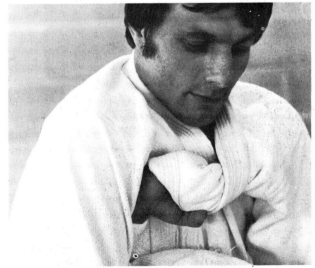

5

Seoi-Otoshi

I will cover the ippon-seoi-otoshi only. When doing morote-seoi-nage you keep hold with both hands and insert the arm under your opponent's armpit. When doing eri-seoi-nage you hold the opponent's lapel on the 'wrong' side, or in other words, both hands holding the same side of the jacket.

With ippon-seoi-nage and ippon-seoi-otoshi there is one very great advantage in the grip. When you take the arm through you control your opponent's arm with both your arms. Therefore, from a basic right side grip you may attack left and the arm you insert under your opponent's left arm controls the left side. You may attack on either side from a left or right grip. A lot of competitors fit their shoulder under their opponent's armpit. This is wrong. The correct

1

2

contact is with the crook of your elbow under your opponent's armpit.

Take a right side grip. Step across with your left foot to outside your partner's left foot. This action should make him think your attack is on the left. 'Switch' through by taking your right leg past your left leg, pivoting on your left foot and bringing your right leg between your left foot and your partner's body. Place your right leg, from the knee to the toes (toes flat) on the mat so the back of your right knee is in contact with the front of your partner's ankle. Your body should make contact as you perform the 'switch' and should maintain contact as you drop on your right lower leg; head tucked in.

This is a throw you can use to 'rescue' a bad ippon-seoi-nage. If you make an ippon-seoi-nage attack which has failed, turn your body to the left and drop onto the left lower leg, tucking sharply and turning to the left. In this case your right lower leg doesn't wrap round your opponent's ankle but is on the ground on the side away from your opponent.

3

4

Okuri-Ashi-Barai

This throw depends on timing. Very little power is required. The opportunity is when your opponent moves sideways, one foot moving towards the other. Many people practise the throw with several sideways steps (this is the method used in nage-no-kata). In a contest it is unusual to have a competitor move in this way. The throw cannot be done against a static opponent, but once you can throw using several steps, reduce the number of steps until you can sweep on the first.

Your leg should be straight and the sole of the foot applied as near the ground as possible. The sweeping leg should 'chase' uke's leg. Your opponent's arm should be controlled on the side you attack but in a contest any opportunity to throw should be taken. If uke puts a hand down and stops the throw, or reduces the score you have lost nothing. Your hand action should be a shallow ⌣.

If you or your opponent crouch the throw is very difficult, if not impossible. If you stand up straight and can get your opponent moving, opportunities will occur. You should work on methods of getting your opponent to step in the direction you require, not only for this technique, but for all others.

1

2

3

Ko-Soto-Gake

1

2

This throw can be used as a 'big' throw, or as a small scorer in which you gain a good advantage in ne-waza.

In order to score ippon you need to draw your opponent so that he steps forward with his right foot in front of your left foot. Use your hands to take him off his left foot and make strong chest to chest contact.

Use your left leg as a hook by placing the back of your bent knee against the back of your opponent's lower leg and lifting, using the whole body and your left leg's hooking movement to throw him to his right back corner.

For the second version, as your opponent places his right foot on the mat, drive off your right foot and hook your left leg in behind your opponent's right leg. Use your body weight and arms to drive your opponent backwards and down, preferably with chest to chest contact. You should finish in a good position for applying a hold down. Beware of falling on your opponent's knee.

3

4

Chapter 16

Renraku-Waza

Earlier in the book, under the heading 'Developing Your Skills' I mentioned the linking of techniques. The following are known as 'combination techniques' because they are methods of linking two throws.

The first attack must be strong enough to get a reaction (preferably a reflex reaction) from your opponent. In some cases you will score with the first attack. In any case you should practise the first throw in isolation. If you got hold of a very hot plate you would drop it automatically. You would not think 'this is hot, I must drop it'. This is a reflex action. If you go to poke someone in the eye with your finger he will blink even if you tell him what you are doing and that you will not actually jab his eye. That is also a reflex. This is the reaction you need for a renraku throw. The first throw, if weak, will not get the desired reaction. These techniques must be practised in free randori against partners who are not aware of what you are practising, after you have reached a reasonable skill level using a co-operative partner. You will soon find out if you have not had enough basic practice.

O-Soto-Gari INTO Ni-Dan-Ko-Soto-Gari

Firstly attack with o-soto-gari. Your partner will either block by preventing you reaping his leg, or trying to 'float' his leg up over your attacking leg. In either case plant your attacking leg firmly on the ground and use the sole of your left foot to reap your partner's left foot off the ground. Contact is on his heel.

The ni-dan-ko-soto-gari must be a reap. To place the sole of the foot against your partner's heel will only enable you to push your partner to the ground. In order to reap his leg out you need a gap to build up the reaping power.

Your o-soto-gari attack must be strong. If you lean back, or fail to break his balance in some way you may be countered with o-soto-gaeshi or even ni-dan-ko-soto-gari, as this throw can also be used as a counter to o-soto-gari. (See page 112.)

1

2 △   3 ▽

4

5

101

Tai-Otoshi INTO
Ko-Uchi-Gari

1

2

The tai-otoshi attack must be strong. In most strong attacks the defender will try to step over your blocking leg. Don't move your left foot, but immediately attack with ko-uchi-gari against the back of his right heel. You must reap. Just placing your foot against his heel when his weight is on it will not work. Ideally the reaping should be a fraction of a second before he places weight on the foot.

You can use eri-tai-otoshi as your first attack by changing your right grip to your partner's right lapel. The advantage with this grip is that the direction of throwing with ko-uchi-gari is much more likely to be correct (to his right-rear corner). If you have to hold the 'wrong' lapel for more than a couple of seconds, you should let go of the sleeve, otherwise you will receive a shido for illegal gripping.

3

4

Ko-Uchi-Gari INTO Seoi-Nage

Make a very strong ko-uchi-gari attack. The usual defence is for the opponent to lift and draw back the attacked leg. Place your attacking leg on the ground. Insert your right arm for ippon-seoi-nage and bring your left foot back into position. Apply ippon-seoi-nage.

The eri-seoi-nage variation can be used. Hold your opponent's right lapel with your right hand. Attack with ko-uchi-gari and repeat the above movements except that your right elbow is tucked under your opponent's right armpit.

Similarly, if you retain your right hand grip you can use morote-seoi-nage.

Use all three methods and see which you prefer. The combination in the photograph sequence is ko-uchi-gari into ippon-seoi-nage. If you have problems ask your instructor to help.

1

2

3

4

5

Uchi-Mata INTO O-Uchi-Gari

Make an uchi-mata attack. Your opponent often pulls back to resist your forward pull. Two important points to remember are:

1. To turn the foot you stand on 90 degrees to the right.

2. To take your opponent down to his rear left corner. If you try to take him directly back he can hop. Similarly, if you take him back to his rear right corner. The leg you attack is a prop. When you take the prop away he should be taken down in that direction. Otherwise he can shift his body weight over the leg not under attack and maintain his balance by hopping. When you convert into o-uchi-gari use your right forearm against your opponent's chest, and curve your body out to your right.

1

2

3

4

5

Chapter 17

Kaeshi-Waza

A counter technique or kaeshi-waza is usually the result of a weak attack. A weak attack is one in which the opponent's balance is not disturbed, or some other element of throwing skill is missing.

When you are attacked you can evade the attack by moving your body in some way, or blocking the attack by using your hips, stomach or arms. Sometimes you can try to push or pull in the opposite direction to that in which the attacker is trying to manoeuvre you. You must be careful when preventing the attack that you are not setting yourself up for a renraku-waza.

Don't over-use counters because this will inhibit your attacking judo. Counters are no use unless your opponent attacks you. If neither of you attack there can be no counters. If you just 'lurk', waiting for a chance to counter, firstly the chance may not come, secondly you may be thrown with renraku-waza, and thirdly you may be penalised for passivity.

When you become more skilled in kaeshi-waza you will find ways in which to tempt your opponent into making a weak attack of the type you wish to counter. Only three examples of kaeshi-waza are given. Your instructor can show you many more.

Remember – when you attack, it is your choice. You decide which throw and whether it will be on the right or left. When you counter-throw, the initiative is taken from you. You must counter the throw your opponent makes, whether it is on the left or right. Therefore it is important to practise counters on both sides.

Harai-Goshi Attack Countered by Te-Guruma

1

This is a good counter because many competitors using harai-goshi do it badly. As your opponent attacks with a (right side) harai-goshi, let go with your left hand. Grip round his right leg (not trousers) and bend your knees. Pin him to you and straighten your knees to lift him off the ground. Rotate him so he turns chest to chest with you and using your arms, wheel him in a circle and drop him in front of you.

This needs some practice and you will benefit from getting your instructor to help. This counter is very spectacular and satisfying to perform. The sequence in brief is:

1. Pin him.

2. Lift him.

3. Turn him.

3

2

4

Harai-Goshi Attack Countered by Utsuri-Goshi

Your opponent attacks with harai-goshi (right side). As he makes his entry let go with your left hand and circle his waist with your arm. (As you are doing this you must bend your knees.) Bounce him up into the air with your hips and stomach, and quickly turn 90 degrees to your left. The trick is getting your hips through before he comes down on his feet. If you have successfully completed this phase you will find you have him on your hips in a left-side o-goshi. Practise both sides.

1

2

The difficulty most people have with this counter is the transition from you on his hip to him on yours. When you bounce him up there must be space for you to make your quarter turn to the left. It must be done very quickly or he will come down onto his feet and you lose the throw. This counter is also a very beautiful one, and very satisfying for the thrower, but it is rarely seen as it is a technique requiring a lot of skill.

4

3

5

O-Soto-Gari Attack Countered by Ni-Dan-Ko-Soto-Gari

Your opponent has made an unsuccessful o-soto-gari attack. You have planted your attacked leg (right) firmly on the mat to prevent his throw. With your hands pin him to your body. Pivot to the right 90 degrees with your right foot and reap your opponent's left heel with the sole of your left foot. As you take him up you arch your back.

Study the pictures on pages 100 and 108. As you are attacked with o-soto-gari, you will find the sequence of ren-rake-waza and kaeshi-waza almost identical.

Uchi-Mata Attack Countered by Tai-Otoshi

This counter is very spectacular when correctly applied.

Your opponent attacks you with a right uchi-mata. Take your left leg back so his sweeping leg passes harmlessly by you. Pivot on your right foot (to the right). Pass your left leg across the front of your opponent's left leg. It helps if you can take his left sleeve as you apply the counter. Don't let go, but try to take a part of the sleeve as well as the normal lapel grip. This prevents uke from blocking the counter by placing his left hand on the mat.

1

2

3

4

Tsuri-Komi-Goshi Attack Countered by Ura-Nage

This is a throw that is not seen often in junior competitions. One problem is that a heavy fall can result, and for this reason a crash mat is a great help in learning the technique and developing confidence in falling from it.

If your opponent attacks you with a throw such as tsuri-komi-goshi, harai-goshi or hane-goshi, you will have the opportunity to apply the throw. It is usually used as a counter-technique.

As your opponent turns in for a right-side attack, let go with your left hand and bend your knees. Wrap your left arm round your opponent's waist and clamp him to you with both hands and arms. Straighten your legs and throw him over your left shoulder as you fall backwards onto the mat.

Don't practise this throw unless your coach says you may, and be very careful while you are practising. Illustrations 4, 5, 6 show the use of a crash mat.

1

2

3

4

5

6

Chapter 18

Kansetsu and Shime-Waza

In some competitions juniors can use armlocks and necklocks if they are over a certain weight. Always find out (if you are over that weight) whether these techniques are allowed, or you could be penalised quite heavily for using them.

If you are a junior (less than 16 years old) never use them even in randori unless your instructor says you may. Never jerk an armlock or necklock. Always let go immediately your partner submits. It is always best to tap your partner in randori or when practising the techniques as tapping the mat may not be noticed by him. In a contest it is simpler because the referee is there to look after your interests and if the mat is tapped the referee will call 'ippon'. If your opponent taps you (or you think he may have tapped you) in a contest, don't let go. Slightly ease off the pressure and if the referee does not make the ippon call carefully re-apply the lock.

1

Ude-Gatame

You opponent is on his back and you are kneeling by his side. He reaches up to grasp your lapel with the hand furthest from you. Take hold of his arm at the elbow, one hand on top of the other. Draw him up onto his side, applying pressure against the elbow. You must curve your back to make a gap between his elbow and your chest. See how many other positions you can find to apply this armlock.

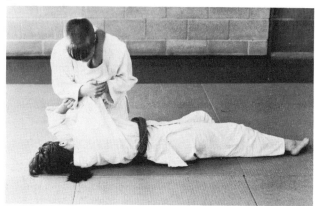

2

Ude-Garami

Bent armlock

This lock is also known as the 'figure four' or 'entangled arm lock'.

Your opponent is on his back and you lie across his chest. His arm is bent (as if he is making the 'koka' signal). Hold his wrist with the hand nearest his head. Thread your other arm under his bicep and place your hand on your own wrist. Rotate his elbow against his wrist. Some people have a great deal of flexibility in their arm. If you find you have difficulties, pull his wrist in towards you and lift his elbow towards his hip.

This lock can also be done with the bent arm reversed. Try it and if you have problems ask your instructor to help.

1

2

Waki-Gatame

Side armlock

With this lock your opponent is on his stomach, or on all fours. Lift the arm nearest to you with his elbow under your armpit. Bear down on the elbow whilst pulling up on the wrist end of the arm. Be careful to apply pressure against the elbow and not the shoulder. There are many ways of applying this lock. See if you can find some.

2

1

3

Hiza-Gatame

Armlock with knee

A good opportunity for this technique is when you are on your back and your opponent is between your legs trying to necklock you, or grasping your collar. (In fact, although you should not try to necklock from between the legs, many people do.)

Take the top arm, just above the wrist with both hands. If his right arm is on top, turn onto your right side and push his left leg away with your right foot. Take your bent left leg over his right elbow and apply pressure with your knee. If you cannot get enough pressure to obtain a submission, place your left fist between your knee and his elbow. This enables you to apply more pressure.

Try to find other ways to apply this lock with your knee.

N.B. The illustrations show the attack on Uke's left elbow.

1

3

2

4

Kata-Juji-Jime

Half cross lock (Photograph 1)

Gyaku-Juji-Jime

Reverse cross lock (Photograph 2)

Nami-Juji-Jime

Normal cross lock (Photograph 3)

The only difference with these three necklocks is in the positioning of the hands. The word 'cross' refers to the arms being crossed. The necklocks are done facing your partner. The grips must be deep (hands touching, or nearly touching, behind your opponent's neck). The thin edges of the wrist must be used – the thumb edge or little finger edge.

When applying the locks, draw the elbows apart as if your arms are a pair of shears or scissors.

1

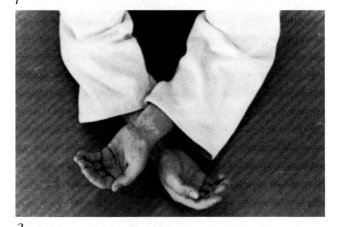

2

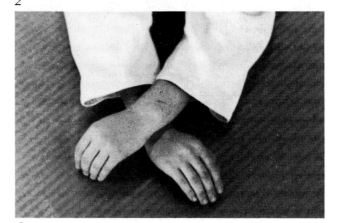

3

The best opportunities in competition are when you are on your back and your opponent is between your legs. If he is on his back and you are astride him it is better to go for tate-shiho-gatame. Be careful not to apply pressure to your opponent's face with these (or any other) necklocks.

A useful way to obtain a cross lock from beneath is to hold your opponent's left lapel with both hands close together. The right hand above the left, thumbs uppermost on both hands. Manoeuvre your opponent so you can slip your right (uppermost) arm over his head and you obtain a strong kata-juji-jime.

4

5

Sode-Guruma

Sleeve wheel

This is a necklock which can be applied from the side or rear of your opponent. First practise against a kneeling or sitting partner and then progress to trying the lock from various supine positions.

Your partner is sitting. Kneel at his right side. Cross your arms. Your left hand reaches across his front and takes the furthest lapel. Your right hand goes behind his head and takes any part of his rear collar or rear jacket (at the top). Apply the lock by drawing the elbows apart as if they are a pair of shears. Again, when you can successfully apply it, practise from various positions, including from the rear.

Sangaku-Gatame

This is an unusual hold for juniors, but is a very powerful one if practised. 'Sangaku' means triangle, and the triangle is formed by hooking one foot behind the other knee.

A good opportunity occurs when you are on your back and your opponent attempts to escape from between your legs by lifting one of your legs onto his shoulder in order to go under that leg.

The photographs show the girl attempting to escape under her opponent's right leg. Hook your right foot in behind your left knee. Roll to your right, taking your opponent over onto her/his back. You will now be in position. Note that the hands and arms are not used to hold, but are placed on the mat above your opponent's head. Do not attempt to apply a necklock.

1

2

3

4

Turning Opponent Over (Face Downwards)

Kneel astride your partner facing his head end. Hold his belt with both hands. Stand and lift, hook both your feet in under your partner and go down again. Slip your right arm under his right armpit and over the back of his neck. Roll to your left taking your partner with you. You should now be on your back and your partner on top of you facing upwards. Keep the arm round the back of the neck and manoeuvre round until you are on top in position for tate-shiho-gatame.

1

2

3

4

5

6

Gradings

A grading is held to decide whether to promote the examinee, and if so, to which grade. The grades are shown on the belt by colour and by the number of red tabs.

Gradings are in two parts. The first part is a demonstration of knowledge and skill and is usually called 'theory'. The second part consists of contests.

It is important that you learn the necessary words, throwing and hold down techniques. However good your contest results are, you cannot be promoted past your theory level.

The syllabus is reviewed every four years and is usually changed, so it is essential to have up-to-date information on what is expected.

The new syllabus will be putting much greater emphasis on technique and theory and it is expected that the competition part of gradings will be taken out at the lower grades.

If you look through your record book you will find the pages which cover your mon grading syllabus. This is where the examiner signs when you complete the theory part of the examination. Make sure that whoever examines you is authorised to do so. They should have a valid examiner's card.

Remember the membership lasts for only one year and you must apply for new membership every twelve months. You should allow two to three weeks for your new membership to be confirmed, so you must apply well before any grading or competition you want to enter, if your membership has run out.

Glossary

Ashi-waza	Leg or foot throws
Chugaeri	Rolling breakfall
Chui	Caution
Dan	Black belt grade
De-ashi-hari(or barai)	Advanced foot sweep throw
Dojo	Judo hall
Eri-soei-nage	Lapel shoulder throw
Gachi	Win
Gari	Reaping
Gyaku-juji-jime	Reverse cross lock
Hajime	Begin
Hane goshi	Spring hip
Hansoku	Disqualification
Hantei	Request for judges' decision on winner
Harai-goshi	Sweeping hip
Hidari	Left
Hikewake	Draw
Hiza-gatame	Armlock using knee
Hiza-guruma	Knee wheel
Hon-kami-shiho-gatame	Basic upper four quarters hold
Hon-tate-shiho-gatame	Basic lengthwise four quarters hold
Hon-yoko-shiho-gatame	Basic side four quarters hold
Ippon	Full point
Ippon-seoi-nage	Single arm shoulder throw
Ippon-seoi-otoshi	Single arm shoulder drop
Jui-jitsu	Flexible art
Judo	Flexible way
Judogi	Judo suit
Judoka	Judo person

Juji-gatame	Straight armlock across the body
Kaeshi-waza	Counter technique
Kake	Throw (final stage)
Kami-shiho-gatame	Upper four quarters hold
Kansetsu-waza	Armlocks
Kata	Pre-arranged judo techniques
Kata-gatame	Shoulder holding
Kata-guruma	Shoulder wheel
Kata-juji-jime	Half cross lock
Katame-waza	Groundwork
Keikoku	Warning
Kesa-gatame	Scarf holding
Koka	Near yuko
Koshi-waza	Hip throws
Ko-soto-gake	Minor outer hook
Ko-soto-gari	Minor outer reaping
Ko-uchi-gari	Minor inner reaping
Kuzure-kami-shiho-gatame	Broken upper four quarters hold down
Kuzure-kesa-gatame	Broken scarf holding
Kuzure-yoko-shiho-gatame	Broken side four quarters hold down
Kuzushi	Breaking the balance
Kyu	Learner grade
Make	Loss
Makura-kesa-gatame	Pillow scarf holding
Ma-sutemi-waza	Rear body sacrifice throws
Matte	Stop
Migi	Right
Mon	Gateway

Morote-seoi-nage	Two arm shoulder throw
Mune-gatame	Chest holding
Nami-juji-jime	Normal cross lock
Ne-waza	Groundwork
Ni-dan-ko-soto-gari	Second stage minor outer reaping
O-goshi	Major hip throw
Okuri-ashi-barai	Sweeping ankle
Okuri-eri-jime	Sliding collar lock
O-soto-gaeshi	Major outer counter
O-soto-gari	Major outer reaping
O-uchi-gari	Major inner reaping
Osaekomi	Holding
Osaekomi-waza	Hold downs
Passivity	You must keep up a series of attacks
Randori	Free practice
Rei	Bow
Renraku-waza	Combination technique
Repêchage	Chance to return (this is a French word).
Sangaku-gatame	Triangular holding
Sasae-tsuri-komi-ashi	Propping-lifting-drawing ankle throw
Shiai	Contest
Shido	Note
Shime-waza	Necklocks
Sode-guruma	Sleeve wheel
Sode-tsuri-komi-goshi	Sleeve lifting drawing hip
Sonomama	Do not move
Soremade	That is all
Sumi-gaeshi	Corner throw
Tachi-waza	Standing judo

Tai-otoshi	Body drop
Tatami	Judo mat
Tate-shiho-gatame	Lengthwise four quarters hold
Te-guruma	Hand wheel
Te-waza	Hand, arm or shoulder throws
Toketa	Holding broken
Tomoe-nage	Circular throw
Tori	Person applying a technique
Tsukuri	Getting into position for a throw
Tsuri-komi-goshi	Lifting drawing hip throw
Uchi-mata	Inner thigh
Ude-garami	Bent armlock
Ude-gatame	Arm crush
Uke	Person receiving a technique
Ukemi	Breakfall
Uki-goshi	Floating hip throw
Ura-nage	Rear throw
Ushiro-kesa-gatame	Rear scarf holding
Utsuri-goshi	Changing hip throw
Waki-gatame	Side armlock
Waza-ari	Near point
Waza-ari-awasete-ippon	Near point; two equal a full point
Yoko-shiho-gatame	Side four quarters hold
Yoko-sutemi-waza	Side body sacrifice throws
Yoshi	Carry on
Yuko	Near waza-ari
Yusei-gache	Superiority win

Grading and Competition Records

Name ....
Instructor ....
Club ....

Kai and Mon Grading Records

GRADE	DATE	VENUE	EXAMINER	GRADE	DATE	VENUE	EXAMINER
1st MON				10th MON			
2nd MON				11th MON			
3rd MON				12th MON			
4th MON				13th MON			
5th MON				14th MON			
6th MON				15th MON			
7th MON				16th MON			
8th MON				17th MON			
9th MON				18th MON			

Competition Record

DATE	VENUE	NAME OF EVENT	WINS	LOSSES	RESULT